LEGENDARY WOMEN SPORTS MEDIA

BY MARTHA LONDON

Book design by Sarah Taplin
Cover design by Sarah Taplin

Photographs ©: Suzanne Vlamis/AP Images, cover (left), 1 (left); Stephen B. Morton/AP Images, cover (right), 1 (right); Library of Congress, 4; John Rooney/AP Images, 6; Adam Scull/PHOTOlink/MediaPunch/IPX/AP Images; 9; Dave Pickoff/AP Images, 11; Bill Greenblatt/UPI/Newscom, 12; Louis Lanzano/AP Images, 15; Matthew Visinsky/Icon Sportswire/AP Images, 17; Kyle Carter/The Neshoba Democrat/AP Images, 19; James D Smith/AP Images, 20; Shutterstock Images, 22; Ann-Sophie Fjello-Jensen/Hashtag Sports/AP Images, 24; Donald Traill/Invision/AP Images, 27; Juan DeLeon/Icon Sportswire/AP Images, 28

Press Box Books, an imprint of Press Room Editions.

ISBN
978-1-63494-280-5 (library bound)
978-1-63494-298-0 (paperback)
978-1-63494-334-5 (epub)
978-1-63494-316-1 (hosted ebook)

Library of Congress Control Number: 2020913882

Distributed by North Star Editions, Inc.
2297 Waters Drive
Mendota Heights, MN 55120
www.northstareditions.com

Printed in the United States of America
012021

About the Author

Martha London works full-time writing children's books. When she isn't writing, you can find her hiking in the woods.

TABLE OF CONTENTS

CHAPTER 1

PIONEERS

On the field, the 1926 Chicago Cubs were terrible. But attendance was rising at home games. Judith Cary Waller played a big role in this. She was manager of the first radio station to regularly air the play-by-play broadcasts of Major League Baseball (MLB) games.

Waller's efforts exposed Chicagoans to baseball without them having to buy tickets. This was especially true for women. Many worked at home while raising children. But in 1926, sales of

Judith Cary Waller managed Chicago's WMAQ, a pioneer in baseball broadcasting.

For years, only men were allowed to enter press boxes at sporting events.

tickets to women skyrocketed. Waller helped bring baseball to everyone.

Sports were long considered an activity for men. Women were often discouraged, or sometimes even banned, from playing. Many people believed sports were improper or even dangerous for women. The same was true for sports media. However, slowly but surely, women began breaking barriers.

While Waller was changing the radio landscape in Chicago, sportswriter Mary Garber was just trying to claim a spot in the press box in North Carolina. In 1946, Garber got a press pass to cover a Duke University football game. She wanted to sit with the rest of the reporters. But Duke's sports information director told her that women were not welcome in the press box. Garber finally gained access months later. She showed the world that women were just as capable as men of writing about sports.

BLACK AND WHITE

Mary Garber did not just pave the way for other female sportswriters. She also worked toward representing Black athletes alongside white ones. In the 1940s and 1950s, many high school and college sports were segregated. Most white reporters did not spend a lot of time talking about Black athletes. But Garber knew that was wrong. She spent time reporting on the basketball games at Winston-Salem State, a historically Black university.

As television's popularity grew, so did the opportunities for women to cover sports. Phyllis George won the Miss America pageant in 1970. In 1975, she joined *NFL Today* on CBS. Some viewers said CBS only hired George for her looks. They thought she should not be a sportscaster because she was a woman. But George wasn't just a pretty face. She worked for CBS Sports for nine years, covering many major events. George's main focus was football. But she also was part of the network's coverage of Triple Crown horse races.

Women were making strides. But female reporters still faced huge barriers. After games, reporters typically go into the locker room to talk to the players. This is an important part

Phyllis George broke barriers when she was hired to work for CBS's weekly NFL pregame show.

of the job. Without it, they wouldn't be able to gather information and insight about the games and players.

In the 1970s, Melissa Ludtke wrote for *Sports Illustrated*. She applied for a press pass to cover the 1977 World Series. As the Series got underway, however, MLB decided women could not enter the locker rooms. This put Ludtke at a disadvantage compared to the male reporters.

Believing this to be unfair, Ludtke sued MLB. Ludtke argued that she could not do her job without equal access to the players. MLB said it wanted to protect its players' privacy. But the court ruled in favor of Ludtke. Teams were required to give all reporters the same level of access, regardless of gender. This allowed Ludtke and the many women who followed

Female reporters who can freely access sports locker rooms have Melissa Ludtke to thank.

to cover sports on equal ground with their male colleagues.

Pioneers, beginning with Waller in the 1920s, paved the way for female sports reporters to come. Women continue to face barriers. But each year, the field of sports reporting becomes more equal.

CHAPTER 2

SETTING A FOUNDATION

Schools weren't required to have girls' sports teams when Christine Brennan was a girl in the 1960s. That never stopped her from playing and writing about sports. Her dad cheered her on as she played with the boys. She also liked to write previews of the weekend's biggest sporting events. Sports and writing were in Brennan's blood.

Brennan started her professional career as a writer in the early 1980s. She pushed the limits wherever she went.

Christine Brennan provided inspiration for many women to advance their careers in sports media.

At the *Miami Herald*, she was the paper's first female sportswriter. At the *Washington Post*, she was the first woman to cover the local pro football team. Today Brennan is best known as an influential columnist for *USA Today*. She's also influential to other female reporters. A scholarship she created has helped more than 175 female sportswriters get their start.

Jackie MacMullan is another ace reporter who worked her way up to influential positions. She spent years at the *Boston Globe*. Her ability to zero in on the heart of a game or series led her to become the *Globe*'s first female columnist. In the early 2000s, she began working for ESPN.

Tennis player Mary Carillo made the jump from the court to the broadcast booth.

ESPN and other TV networks have provided new opportunities for women. Breaking in was a slow process, though. Mary Carillo was one of the first to get on TV. After retiring from tennis in 1980, she was hired as a TV analyst. Her inside knowledge gave her an edge over other reporters. This made her a go-to source for information on women's and men's tennis matches.

Doris Burke got her start at ESPN in 1991. Some men complained about hearing a woman talking about basketball. Burke responded by working even harder. Fans grew to respect her

LESLEY VISSER

For any major sporting event, chances are Lesley Visser was the first woman to cover it. She began at the *Boston Globe* in 1974, where she became the paper's first female pro football writer. During the 1980s, she moved into television. From there, she covered numerous major sporting events, including the Super Bowl and the Olympics. She's also the only woman to be inducted into the Pro Football Hall of Fame.

ESPN basketball reporter Doris Burke is one of the most respected broadcasters in the United States.

insightful basketball analysis. Now she's one of the most trusted voices in the network's basketball coverage.

No show has been more important to ESPN than *SportsCenter*. Fans have been turning to it for daily recaps and analysis since 1979. The anchors' personalities are a big part of the show's appeal. Gayle Gardner was an anchor in the early 1980s. Fans quickly learned they could trust her as much as the male anchors. This helped create opportunities for more women.

In 1990, Robin Roberts became ESPN's first Black anchorwoman. She started on an overnight version of *SportsCenter*. Over her 15 years she worked her way to the important prime-time edition.

Nobody has anchored *SportsCenter* longer than Linda Cohn. Since 1992, she's connected with fans through her humor and passion for sports.

Pam Oliver looked up to Roberts early in her career. Now many young female journalists

Linda Cohn has entertained and informed ESPN viewers as a longtime *SportsCenter* anchor.

19

reach out to Oliver for advice. That's because Oliver has been a trusted source as a football sideline reporter since 1995.

Sideline reporting takes unique skills. Pioneers such as Oliver, Andrea Kremer, Suzy Kolber, and Michele Tafoya needed great reporting and interviewing skills. But they also needed to be sharp and fast, and they had to be able to report from loud and tricky spots. These women helped make their role essential for fans and opened the doors for many women to follow.

Pam Oliver made a name for herself as one of the best NFL sideline reporters in the business.

CHAPTER 3

NEW MEDIA, NEW ERA

Young and charismatic, Erin Andrews began her sportscasting career in 2000. Her positive attitude made it easy for athletes to talk to her on the sideline. Andrews got her break covering college football. Her knowledge of a wide range of sports led her to cover many major events, including the World Series. However, she's best known for her work on football. Fox Sports calls on Andrews as a key member of its top broadcast team for pro football.

Erin Andrews has covered a variety of sports for ESPN and FOX Sports.

From left, Katie Nolan and Mina Kimes are rising stars in the modern era of sports journalism.

Sports media in the 2000s began to change. Newspaper and TV jobs were still important. But the internet opened up many new opportunities in sports coverage. Reporters and analysts could work across multiple mediums. Several women took advantage of these opportunities to help bring fans closer than ever to the action.

Mina Kimes exemplifies this shift. As an investigative reporter for ESPN, Kimes tackles hard subjects head-on. But Kimes also hosted the *ESPN Daily* podcast. Podcasts are similar to radio programs, but they are prerecorded instead of live. In 2020, Kimes transitioned away from the podcast. ESPN installed Kimes as one of its new analysts on *NFL Live*.

In an industry that's still predominantly white, Jemele Hill introduced new perspectives with her outspoken and unflinching style. In 2006, Hill joined ESPN as a columnist.

A SIDE OF COMEDY

Katie Nolan knows how to make people laugh. She also knows her sports. Before she was on national television, though, she was in her living room. She got her start talking about sports on YouTube. Television producers from Fox noticed her. On Fox, and later on ESPN, Nolan hosted comedic TV shows. She hasn't left the online world entirely. She continues to produce humorous podcasts and web shows.

She eventually became one of the few Black female sportscasters. As *SportsCenter* anchors, she and Michael Smith offered unique views on athletes and sports, often from a Black perspective.

Hill does not turn away from difficult topics, including racism. She believes it is part of her job to make pro sports more equal. In 2018, Hill left ESPN and began writing for the *Atlantic*, a news magazine. But she didn't leave sports behind. Hill continues to comment on racism and social justice issues in sports.

Jessica Mendoza isn't about to stop breaking barriers. The two-time Olympic medalist in softball found a home as a sportscaster and analyst. With her experience

Jemele Hill isn't afraid to take a strong stand on issues that matter to her.

as an outfielder at the top levels of softball, Mendoza was able to offer unique perspectives about that sport.

Baseball coverage had almost always been left to men. But Mendoza began breaking down those barriers. In 2015, she became the first woman to call a baseball game as an analyst for ESPN. The next season, she was part of ESPN's regular broadcast team for *Sunday Night Baseball*. Working alongside former baseball stars, she showed her voice was just as insightful. Mendoza continued making history in 2020, when she became the first woman to serve as a solo analyst for national baseball coverage.

Jessica Mendoza talks with Houston Astros executive Reid Ryan before a game in 2017.

MILESTONES

1926
Judith Waller manages the first station to broadcast a regular schedule of Major League Baseball games.

1946
Mary Garber becomes the first woman to regularly gain access to the press box.

1981
Christine Brennan is the first female sports reporter for the *Miami Herald*.

1992
Linda Cohn becomes an anchor on *SportsCenter*. She goes on to become the longest-serving anchor in the history of the show.

2018
Aly Wagner, a retired US women's national soccer team star, is the first woman to call the men's World Cup on national TV.

2020
Mina Kimes, a Korean American sportscaster, joins ESPN's *NFL Live!*

GLOSSARY

analysts
People who explain details about a certain topic.

anchor
A person who leads a television news show.

charismatic
Charming and engaging.

columnist
A person who writes opinion stories.

press pass
A badge that allows a member of the media access to the field, press box, or locker room.

segregated
Separate or set apart based on race, sex, or religion.

sued
Took legal action against a person or institution.

TO LEARN MORE

To learn more about legendary women in sports media, go to **pressboxbooks.com/AllAccess**. These links are routinely monitored and updated to provide the most current information available.